ADVERTISING
Initiation Guide

Agustin Medina

INDEX

Historical Background

First advertising agencies

1 Structures and business relationships

1.1 Marketing and Advertising

1.2 The advertising agency

1.3 Client-Agency Relationships

Annex: Total media ad spending worldwide

2 Development of the advertising campaign

2.1 The "Briefing"

2.2 The strategy

2.3 Creativity

2.4 Research

Annex: Theory of Creativity

HISTORICAL BACKGROUND

Many people maintain that advertising has existed since time inmemorial. Even in Egyptian hieroglyphs you can make out merchants offering products.

If advertising is regarded as a promotional vehicle for a product or a service, then it's true that the history of advertising began when someone offered goods orally or through printed media, although it was printed on the frieze of an Egyptian temple or on a marble slab on the streets of the ancient city of Ephesus 500 years before Christ.

In the ruins of this city, the birthplace of the great philosopher Heraclitus, you can still see a marble stone on the main street with a few graphics that indicated the nearby presence of a brothel. Undoubtedly this would qualify as an advertisement; it has all the features of the advertising message.

However, in this book we will not talk about the history of advertising, but about contemporary advertising as we know it today.

The first modern advertising ads appear in the mid-seventeenth century, at the same time as the first newspapers appeared. They described the crafts of different artisans or hotel establishments and catering businesses, but the format was very primary, given that they were basically texts like those we can find in classified advertising sections in newspapers nowadays.

First advertising agencies

In the mid-nineteenth century the modern brand concept appeared, and with it came the first traces of the modern advertising industry.

Initially there were agents who acted as intermediaries between advertisers and newspapers. They were responsible for developing the advert, taking it to the newspaper and, after its publication, billing and charging the client. As compensation for their work they received a discount from the media channel, with the advertiser only being charged the price of the fare. Therefore the service for the client was free.

The first reported agent is Volney B. Palmer, who opened an office in Philadelphia in 1841. In Spain it was Rafael Roldós Viñolas, who in 1872 founded Centro de Anuncios in Barcelona; a company that went on to become Roldós Advertising agency, which remains active to this date in the market.

The success of agents and advertising was stunning throughout the world and advertising agencies as we understand them today started to emerge. Some of them, such as McCann-Erickson and J. Walter Thompson, among others, have been in the market for over a hundred years.

Also in the mid-nineteenth century, notorious brands that are still very important today exist, such as Procter & Gamble, which was created in 1837.

In 1886 Coca Cola is born. Given its significance in the market, this can be considered as the true beginning of modern advertising. Coca Cola adverts from those days already have a modern format wherein text, graphics and image form an indivisible whole.

STRUCTURES AND BUSINESS RELATIONSHIPS

1.1   Marketing and Advertising

While the emergence of marketing as a concept came much later than that of advertising, you could say that advertising is a part of marketing.

In the definition of marketing, the whole process of commercializing a product is included since its creation until its consumption. This process involves a multitude of factors that the success or failure of the commercial product depend on to a greater or lesser extent. These are disciplines that, put together, constitute the so-called "marketing mix". One of these disciplines is advertising which, given its decisive force in the process, has achieved a high degree of specialization and possesses autonomy outside the advertising company, meaning it has its own area of development in advertising agencies.

Despite this apparent detachment, advertising agencies are completely subordinated to marketing, as all their work is determined by the latter's requirements and the instructions received from it at all times.

In modern companies that operate in the field of consumer products, the marketing department coordinates and, in a way, directs the activity of other departments as important as R & D (research and development), manufacturing, distribution, sales, advertising departments, promotion, public relations and merchandising. In fact, those responsible for products and brands, known as Product Managers and Brand Managers, work under the leadership of the Marketing Director.

They set the guidelines for the research of new products and they project the manufacturing of the company's different products. They're also responsible for stimulating the distribution channels and finding new channels for the future, they coordinate sales policies, advertising objectives and public relations and design the promotion and merchandising strategies. In conclusion, they look after the whole process of a product's life, from its birth to its death.

"Brand Manager" and "Product manager"

Every product sold by a company has its own brand. But often a brand encompasses different products within a same consumption area. (For example: Danone is a yogurt name, but it's also the name of many other different dairy products. Rexona is the name of a solid deodorant and other spray deodorants, but it's also an antiperspirant and a type of soap. The Hyundai brand is the same for different car models: Sonata, Eantra, Accent, Coupe, Atos, etc.)

The Brand Manager, reporting directly to the Marketing Director, is responsible for the commercial benefits of all products with a same brand or, when the products have different brands, is responsible for all products in the same area of consumer goods (cosmetics, cleaning, food, etc.).

The Product Manager, under the direct orders of the Brand Manager, is responsible for managing the commercial benefits of a product or products that may or may not have the same brand. Within the same company a Product Manager may be responsible for products that correspond to various Brand Managers. The Product Manager is the last piece and, to some extent, the key part of the marketing department of the company, because he maintains a more direct contact, given that he is the coordinator of everything that affects the company's products, with all departments involved in the marketing process. In the area of advertising, which, as we have mentioned, possesses autonomy from the company, the Product Manager maintains the day-to-day relationship with the agency, setting goals and evaluating their work.

Advertising and communication directors.

In service companies and others with a unique brand and product, there isn't a marketing department which is as complete as the one described in the previous section, based on large consumer products companies. On various occasions, a Marketing Director, assisted by a small department, is responsible for coordinating all the tasks listed, but without direct power over some of the company's important activities.

Some companies also include the figure of an Advertising Director to be directly responsible for all matters relating to this activity and relationships with agencies. Also, in the case of companies with large institutional influences in their communications, such as banks, it's the director of communications who takes on these responsibilities.

R & D (Research and Development)

Companies are increasingly aware that the life cycle of products are becoming shorter. It is estimated that 9 out of 10 brands currently on the market will be gone within ten years. And if one looks back, most of the brands we use today did not exist ten years ago. Thus, the development of new products and new brands is an obligation for every business that wishes to remain alive in the coming years.

This is why R & D departments are like laboratories where new products are studied in order to adapt them to new consumer demands.

Companies also develop other types of research regarding products and markets. In the case of advertising, this research is conducted outside the company by specialized institutes. These institutes work with known social research techniques and consumer studies that keep marketing managers informed on buyer motivations and consumer preferences regarding the company's and the competitors' products.

Likewise, using systems such as Nielsen you can get a feel for market movements and possible buyer trends. These institutes are also used for pre-tests and post-tests for advertising campaigns, to test packaging, brands, new product formulas, etc. Research institutes are very important for marketers, allowing them, where possible, to eliminate risks in all actions to be taken with their products.

Manufacturing

Although the factory itself, in terms of the physical and final execution of the products depends on the chemical experts, engineers, etc. who run everything, the entire work is determined by the demands of those who run the marketing of the company. These propose experimenting with new formulas, determine the choice of the formula based on the ingredients, quality and costs, and suggest the packaging or labeling systems. They also decide the quantity to be manufactured of each product at all times. Everything is controlled and coordinated by the Product Manager in charge of each of the products.

Distribution

There are many different ways to distribute a product or, in other words, getting it from the producer to the consumer; a very long road that sometimes increase the initial cost of the product by 50 per cent.

Some companies, such as Avon, offer home delivery of their products through a wide network of in-house sales staff, therefore assuring that they go directly from the manufacturer to the consumer. Other companies use a mail distribution system. And now e-commerce is revolutionizing distribution methods. But as of today, the vast majority of companies that sell consumer products continue to use traditional channels: wholesalers and retailers.

Wholesalers buy products from a company (the manufacturer) to sale them to another company (the retailer). They work with very little profit margin, which is compensated by the large number and variety of products they sell. They only work with fast-selling products and they purchase from many different manufacturers and different products, often even purchasing competitive products. Given the scale of their purchases they obtain very low prices from manufacturers.

There are also purchasing cooperatives formed by retailers to obtain the same prices and payment terms from manufacturers as big wholesalers.

Retailers are businesses that sell directly to the consumer and are supplied by wholesalers, cooperatives, or in many cases directly from the manufacturer.

Sales

The sales department or sales network has the mission of contacting directly with wholesalers and retailers to make the distribution and sales policy successful. The head of this department is the National Sales Manager, who is responsible for implementing the objectives of the company's sales and recruiting salespeople; there are also Regional Delegates, with the same functions as the national director but in specific areas of the country; and Supervisors, who are under the control of Regional Delegates and are responsible for a number of salespeople, who they form and direct. They are also responsible for contacting with major wholesalers in their area; salespeople, who work directly with wholesalers and retailers, and are also responsible for promoting the display of the product at the point of sale.

Advertising

Generally, an advertising department as such doesn't exist within a company, although there are some companies that incorporate one, and even put together their own advertising agency, which only handles products from the company itself. Usually, however, given the importance of advertising in the marketing mix of a product, companies put their advertising in the hands of specialized companies (advertising agencies), with which they maintain a constant, intimate relationship.

Even in companies with their own advertising department, it is common to turn to independent agencies for large campaigns.

Public relations

It is increasingly common for companies to put their institutional public relations in the hands of specialized companies, with the aim of projecting a positive image of the company or brand through communication actions that go beyond the scope of paid advertising, in order to appear in the editorial content of the media. The goal is to have an active presence in all sectors of communications that relate to the life of the company and its products or services, from an economic projection of corporate governance to the personal image of the management.

Everything contributes towards consumers forming a compelling vision of the company and, as a consequence, influencing the final sale of their products.

Sales Promotion

This is another task of the marketing department and it consists in carrying out very specific actions supporting sales of products in certain situations. These actions are conducted by the marketing department (Product Manager and Brand Manager) in collaboration with promotional marketing agencies, and will be one of the specific topics of one of the chapters in this book.

Merchandising

Merchandising is the activity carried out inside the selling point with the aim of showing and promoting the product better than any of the competitors. Like other marketing activities, it is also planned by the Brand or Product Manager and executed by the sales department, sometimes in collaboration with specialized companies.

1.2 The Advertising Agency

The classic diagram of an advertising agency has five key departments: creative, customer service, media, accounting and coordination or traffic. Each is headed by an Executive Director who reports to the CEO of the agency.

The General Manager

The General manager, or CEO, of an advertising agency primarily serves three specific missions:

- Establish, maintain and monitor relationships with

prospects (potential customers).

-Develop and oversee the public relations plan of the agency.

- Exercise the normal functions of any other type of enterprise (contact with heads of departments, economic policies, etc.).

In most agencies, especially multinationals, there is also the figure of the President, who maintains the institutional relations of the agency and shares the management of the economic guidelines and tasks to strengthen the public image of the company with the CEO.

The Creative department

It is the heart of the agency. This department carries out the specific work on which the whole activity of an advertising agency revolves around: the advertising campaign.

Every campaign is created and performed by a team made up of a copywriter and an art director. This team is called the Creative Group. In an agency there are several of these groups that are coordinated and supervised by one or more Creative Directors, heads of departments and managers to maintain the level of creativity that gives character to the agency.

To develop their activity, these groups cooperate with different services within the Creative Department:

a) Graphic Production, which is responsible for all the infrastructure related to the production for printed media (budgets, photographers, models, artwork, etc.) and technical supervision of the printing of different materials.

b) Audiovisual Production, responsible for the infrastructure related to audiovisual media (video and film budgets, radio recordings, etc.).

The Clients Services department

Also called the Accounts Department is responsible for maintaining the direct relationship with customers. It gathers information and prepares it to be delivered to the Creative Groups. In large agencies, members of this department (Account Managers and Executives) correspond, on a hierarchial level, to the client's Brand Managers and Product Managers. And its organization within the agency, in relation to the customers they manage, is equivalent to the marketing team of the client with regards to its products.

Thus, the Client Services Manager is responsible for all the agency's clients; Account Managers are responsible in turn for a broad group of customers, and Executives have a responsibility over one or more clients, depending on their importance.

The members of this department act as representatives of the client within the agency and, as such, serve as liaisons and coordinate with other departments in all matters related to the clients they manage (preparing campaigns, research studies, budgets, billing, etc.). In most traditional agencies, people in the accounts department are responsible for presenting and selling the agency's creative product to the client.

The Media department

It is responsible for planning the distribution of the advertising campaign in different media channels. It also acts as a liaison between the agency and the media, passing on the necessary orders for the publication of adverts. It also assesses the effectiveness of campaigns, measuring the levels of coverage and frequency.

Today, many advertisers plan and buy their media through specialized companies, called Central Media. In these cases, they use the agency's Media department as a consultant to contrast different points of view.

The Finance department

As with any other business, this department of the advertising agency is responsible for managing finance, bookkeeping and controlling the billing, cash and payments, taxes, payroll, social security, etc...

The Traffic department

It is a separate department whose primary mission is to coordinate the relationship between the Customer

Service department and the Creative department. It carries out the planning for deadlines on every project, verifies its compliance and also controls the costs of these for billing purposes. Its work is especially useful in large agencies.

1.3 Agency/Client Relationship

Advertising agencies maintain relationships with two types of customers: potential (prospects) and real customers. In the first case, the relationship is oriented to converting the prospect in a real client of the agency. The responsibility of this relationship with prospects is directly that of the agency director, who, if there is no New Business department, is also responsible for maintaining it.

The intermediate steps that define this relationship are:

- Initial contact through a phone call, personal letter, brochure, video, website, etc.
- Periodic mailings of information on philosophy and activities of the agency.
- Visit of the client to the agency
- Speculative campaign

The relationship with the real clients is determined by the daily work. This work begins with a briefing provided by the client and, theoretically, ends when work is showed in the media and billed to the customer.

The work in each of its stages of development (roughs, sketches, artwork) is submitted by the agency to the client and must be approved by him before taking the next step. Those responsible for these submissions and approvals are Account Executives, on the agency's behalf, and Product Managers, on the client's, with the supervision of the respective Account Managers and Brand Managers.

Depending on each agency, or the importance of the presentations, they can be passed on to the creative agency staff, although even in these cases, the Account Executive continues to act as the coordinator.

Remuneration system

Conventional advertising agencies of some importance, international or not, are billing the client on the basis of a percentage of the total investment budget of each of its customers. This percentage pays all agency services, from creative work to media planning and buying.

Also, in some cases, agencies bill for their services through a fee (monthly fixed amount) or by an individual assessment of each specific job.

When the agency charges the customer the percentage of the investment in the media budget, it delivers the client all kinds of discounts received from the media.

Ethics on competitive products

Unless authorized by each of them, an agency can not simultaneously take on two different customer accounts belonging to the same area of competence. This prevents information from leaking that can influence the development of campaigns.

However, when a customer decides to stop working with an agency, the agency can take over the advertising of its nearest competitor, taking advantage of the experience gained in the product's field.The information that the agency has from briefings must be treated as a seal of confession to avoid the competition from knowing the marketing plans of the previous client. This is very important since the professional future of the agency and of each of its members depends on it.

Special Services

In addition to the services of an advertising agency, these tend to provide their customers with a range of special services among which the most important are:

- Prepare salespeople, wholesalers and retailers conventions.

- Create audiovisual products for presentations.

- Design stands for fairs and exhibitions.

- Decorate shop windows.

- Public relations / press releases.

- Brand design and corporate image development.

For most of these services clients hire specialized companies, but sometimes they demand it from the advertising agency, which will always be willing to provide it.

DEVELOPMENT OF THE ADVERTISING CAMPAIGN

2.1 The "briefing"

The briefing is a basic tool in an advertising agency to build the strategy, creativity and media planning for all advertising campaigns. It is a compendium of information about the product and the company, which the agency receives before starting the implementation of the campaign.

The Product Manager is responsible for elaborating the briefing, with the support of several companies specializing in auditing markets, in order to obtain the necessary data to analyze the evolution of their products.

A good briefing must contain all the information that the customer has about the market, product, competition, distribution, consumer, target group and marketing and advertising goals.

The following are, for example, some of the main points that a briefing must contain, but its relevance depends on the type of each product or service.

The market

The basic information required on the market is:

- Total market volume in monetary value and product units.

- Distribution of sales by geographical areas.

- Distribution of sales during the year.

- Market share in percentages of the different brands on the market.

- If the market is steady, declining or evolving.

Product

- Characteristics and performance.

- Main use of the product.

- Test results of the product against competition. (Advantages and disadvantages)

- Packaging.

- Price.

- Current position in the market (market share). - Distribution and sales by geographical areas.

Competition

- Analysis of advertising and proposals that each brand makes to the consumers.

 -Media investments and seasonality.

 - Sales promotions.

- Strengths and weaknesses.

Distribution

- What channels of distribution does the product use from the factory to the consumer?

- Does the company have a network of in-house salespeople or do they use multibrand agents?

- What kind of store sells more?

Consumer

- Who is the consumer?

- Age

- Sex

- Marital status

- Social class

- Educational level

- Habitat

- Habits (How do they use the product? How often?)

-Motivations for the use of the product

- Attitude towards the product

The "target group" (target audience)

The public who we wish to sell the product to is not necessarily always the same group that is consuming the product.

- Who should we direct the marketing communication at?
- Is it a buyer or a consumer? (Housewives buy many products to be consumed by other family members.)

- Age, sex, marital status, etc.

-Style of life and behavior.

The Objectives of marketing and advertising

Marketing goals are quantitative, and are expressed in numbers and percentages; the advertising goals are qualitative and are expressed in terms of communication.

- Market share objective in the short, medium and long term. (Marketing)

- Net advertising investment. (Marketing)

- What should the content of the communication be? What do we want to communicate about the product or service? (Advertising)

  - What is the desired consumer response? How do we expect the consumer to respond to the advertising message? (Advertising)

A good briefing must answer these questions without being exhaustive. All of the agency's subsequent work depends on its clarity and accuracy and, therefore, so does the quality and success of the campaign.

2.2 The strategy

From the client's briefing, the agency develops a communication strategy and a plan is defined to achieve the marketing and advertising objectives that have been marked. This plan should encourage the consumer and provoke a positive response from him, culminating in a buying action.

The agency rethinks the client briefing, analyzes and calls into question each and every one of its points, adding its experience in other markets. Because sometimes, when you're too close to the problem, you can't analyze it clearly. A new vision, a new perspective can give us the key to solving a problem that seemed unsolvable.

In my particular experience, I have two cases that perfectly illustrate this theory. The first is the Schweppes tonic campaign "Man of the tonic" (Bernard Lecoq), which I co-authored and, together with Jorge Garcia, chose the character, I defined the strategy and personally wrote the first five scripts of the series of television spots.

The marketing department from Schweppes had defined in its briefing that the target audience should be young people between fifteen and eighteen, because this agegroup encompasses the greatest consumers of soft drinks. However, the agency, examining the data supplied by the client, concluded that tonic was an adult beverage because of the taste and social status of the product, and should be sold to a wider audience above the age of twenty one. Finally, this decision was made, and the success of one of the most famous advertising campaigns of the Spanish market proved that the agency was right.

Also, when we launched the first 4x4 Suzuki Samurai car, the agency had to fight for almost a year to convince the client that the target audience should be urban youth, rather than farmers, and to prove that it was more interesting to position the car as a vehicle for leisure, rather than as a work tool.

Now it seems obvious that it should be so; but from the perspective of the customer, the Suzuki Samurai was a perfect substitute for a Land Rover, which, with the entry of Nissan Patrol in the market had lost 50 per cent of its sales.

The communication strategy prepared by the agency compiled an entire set of arguments to develop a plan of action in order to accomplish all the objectives of the briefing. The strategy explains how to act from a strict communication point of view to get the right response from consumers, and also what the creative strategy of the campaign will be, what materials will form its cored in the media and how the budget will be distributed across the different actions contemplated.

Each agency has a different way of developing its strategy. In some cases, there is a Planner, a kind of director of strategy who is responsible for its preparation. In other cases, the agency has a strategy committee that is usually formed by the senior management of the agency. And it is often the accounts department (Account Managers and Client Service Manager) who are responsible for carrying it out. In any case, it is an important task which will affect all of the agency's subsequent work and, especially, the creative development of the campaign.

2.3 Creativity

The Creative Group

If we go back to the beginnings of organized advertising, we can see that the Copywriter is a person that works alone and only comes into contact with the other workers (illustrators, designers, photographers, etc.) when he has to translate his ideas into a rough draft.

This system meant that agencies depended on the genius of an individual rather than the work of a team. The team (cartoonists, designers, etc.) were limited to graphically developing ideas from the Copywriter that were not their ideas and in which they had not participated. To some extent, the agency was using only fifty percent of the capacity of many creative people, as they were required only for manual labor, almost without giving them the opportunity to intervene in the area of ideas.

Later on, the idea that several heads think better that one became widespread in agencies, and they decided to use the creative talent of their artists and designers and convert them into what are now called Art Directors. These Art Directors were asked to form a team with a Copywriter for the creation of ideas, making the most of the ability of two individuals from different backgrounds (one skilled in spoken and written language, the other an expert in visual language) obtaining a less partial and more comprehensive vision of ideas.

Actually the team today is usually formed by two people: an Art Director and a Copywriter; two people, always working together on each problem-usually at the same desk-, build an understanding and freedom of expression that greatly favors the creative work. This team is called the 'Creative Team" in agencies.

The "Creative Team", working under the orders of a Creative Director, is directly responsible for developing the campaign. They receive customer briefings and strategies prepared by the agency, and from there they create creative concepts and develop the rough-drafts that will later be presented to the client.

Concepts and roughs-draft

The concept is the basic idea from which the campaign will be developed and should be a perfect synthesis of the strategy. The concept results in an initial work material called rough-draft, and that is a first approach of what the advert will go on to be. The rough-draft is a material that is used internally by the agency, but sometimes it is presented to the client, if the client is professional enough to understand it.

At the beginning of a campaign, the Creative Team often develops several alternative concepts, which are examined by the Creative Director, who selects some of them to be developed at a rough draft level. The specific function of the rough-draft is to demonstrate that the concept can be encoded without difficulty in each of the media channels where the campaign will appear. In advertising, the term rough-draft has become so common that it is also used to refer to anything (text, drawing, illustration, etc.) that is barely developed.

Final sketches

From the rough-draft, and once it has been approved by internal agency committees, the sketches are developed, trying to achieve a true reflection of what the ad will be once it's in the media. The greater or lower completion of the sketches, which range from a simple drawing and a text to a photo and figurative real text, depends on the client that must judge the work and their ability to understand it. Nowadays, with computers, presentations are completely finished, almost as they will be later shown in the media.

In audiovisual media, a radio sketch is called a script, or a story board in the case of television or video.

The lay-out

The lay-out is the form in which the various elements are laid out in the ad:

- Typography: all the text that is in the ad.

- Graphics: artwork, photos and illustrations .

- Brand: product name.

- Logo: the particular design of the brand.

  - Symbol: the graphics that sometimes accompany a product logo. 2.4

2.4 Research

During the process of carrying out an advertising campaign there are different moments when research has an important role. Firstly, research is the support of a good briefing and a good strategy: research on the product, on the market, on consumers and on competition. Quantitative research and motivational research should be done a priori by the client to get to know their own products and what consumers think about them.
Later, the agency conducts its own qualitative research through focus groups with consumers, in order to contrast the information received from the client.
These meetings are held with eight or nine people from the target audience and are moderated-usually by a specialist, a sociologist in charge of directing the conversation towards the planned topics.

When the creative team has done its work, and before starting the final stage of production of the materials, it is common to perform a pre-test to see if there are elements that are difficult to understand or negative for the consumer.

And finally, when the campaign has been released in the media, post-tests that quantitatively measure the levels of visibility and understanding of the messages of the campaign are carried out.

ANNEX

THEORY OF THE CREATIVITY

Creativity is a leap over logic. It is a way of overcoming the barriers that limit our ability to associate elements or ideas. With logic we can move from a rose to a garden, from the garden to the house, from the house to its inhabitants; from the people (through their chores) we can move to other areas which are increasingly distant from a rose: administrative (office), student (college), engineer (factory), marine merchant (sea).

Creative thinking allows us to abandon this system of immediate associations and go directly from a rose to the sea: rose and sea, two distant elements in space and time, but nearby thanks to an act of imagination which we have reached directly without a logical process.

Creative acts take elements away from their surroundings through the imagination and relate them to other elements from different fields.

The imagination is a creative way of using thought, but it isn't an act of creation in itself. Because the act of creation demands that a thought materializes by producing an innovation. And relating things in different contexts is, by definition, an incomplete act (rose and sea), starting a journey that only becomes authentic creation when the two elements come together to shape a new concept or a new form or a new image: a sea of roses.

Although the imagination is a way of creating and sometimes materializes in a creative act, this is not always is the case. Imagination can also potentially be developed into a merely imaginative act and not creating an implicit innovation.

A rose floating in the sea is an example of an imaginative act, the result of a process of imagination (the relation between two different elements in a framework and context), but no innovation is derived from it, given the fact that a floating rose in a sea is nothing new. It's something that logic (not of thought but of action) can come up with at any time. A woman wearing a rose pinned to her hair swimming in the sea; the rose falls off and drifts away from the woman floating in the water, etc. It is a fact that has already occurred a thousand times, or which is likely to occur at any time. It doesn't introduce anything new in the filed of behavior, nor is it a new concept of a rose or the sea (the rose is still a rose, and the sea is still the sea); neither is it a new, distinct, different, unusual image.

However, a sea of roses is not an event that may occur within the realms of logic. It is a new image, a new form of a rose and the sea, a new concept of each of the elements: in short, an innovation and, therefore, a creative act that, like the rose floating in the sea, has emerged from an identical creative process in both cases.

Creativity is our ability to put strange objects in relation with each other, establishing a new and original relationship between them; our ability to imagine new solutions to old problems; our ability to surprise, in the case of advertising, the receptors of our messages.

CREATIVITY

3.1 The world of ideas

The essence of advertising work is creativity. And creativity is to come up with ideas that redefine things. Publicists spend their lives redefining things; looking for new approaches, new angles from which to look at reality with new eyes; trying to find original definitions for everyday things.

Tomato juice can turn into blood if we put a Band-aid on top. A hairdryer can become a gun only by putting it against someones temple. Everything's meaning changes when we look at it from a new perspective. Creative ideas are a leap above logic, linking different concepts, - a tomato and a Band-aid, a hairdryer and our temple - to give way to a new concept, a new image capable of surprising and connecting with our emotions, breaking the barrier of our rationality.

Classical ideas and innovative ideas

In the world of ideas, there are different kinds and not all have the same value. It's the same as in the arts; there are always at least two schools: the classical and the avant-garde. The classic is easier to understand, due to its more orthodox patterns: the proportions of the human body in the Greek and Roman sculptures, the realism in painting before the twentieth century, etc. However, the avant-garde implies a revolution, breaking schemes and patterns: abstract art painting or minimalist sculptures are two good examples.

It is the same in advertising. There are classic ideas and innovative ideas. Classical schemes are well known, such as detergent TV adverts, whose scripts always respond to the sequence "problem -product - solution": the child's dirty shirt that has to be cleaned to attend a birthday party, and thanks to product X, the shirt ends up being spotless and the child has a great time at his friend's party. Many TV adverts for consumer products follow this pattern.

The same occurs with other classic schemes, such as a speaker / presenter in radio, or the graphical disposition in the layout of a head line, photo, copy and slogan in many print ads.

The ideas that respond to a classical scheme are easy to conceive and to implant, because they have already been created and performed many times. They require more graft than creativity and they don't always work, because the receptor already knows the game and can not be surprised or shocked by it. They are closer to information than advertising, and their level of creativity is extremely low.

However, innovative ideas are difficult to conceive and to carry out, because there are no antecedents. They are also difficult to investigate because they do not conform to known consumer experiences. And above all, they are difficult to sell to customers, because they require large doses of intuition to believe them. But it's worth the effort to find new ideas, because they always surprise the consumer, they stay etched in people's memories, and when they're truly brilliant and different, they lead to sales growing dramatically.

3.2 Creative techniques

Without going into the debate of whether a creative person is born creative, or if is possible to learn how to become creative, we can confirm that there are techniques that can increase our creativity. These techniques teach us to use our imagination and think in a different way. They help us to find solutions, which would be very difficult to reach through conventional ways. And their applications are valid for multiple fields of activity, from scientific research to advertising.

The multidisciplinary group

This technique, also known as Brain Storming, is one of the most common and is developed by groups of people from different disciplines. This is to avoid the expert and to compel each individual to use plain language when trying to explain to others a subject of expertise. The multidisciplinary group, according to Kaufmann, Fustier and Drevet stimulates the imagination of its components. It is an inexhaustible reservoir of ideas, and the knowledge of each person at the time of application has a cumulative effect; that is, the findings are obtained in a greater number than could be obtained adding the individual findings.

The optimal number of participants or members of the group is from 8 to 10, half of whom are experts in the topic and for the other half different profiles from other areas are chosen. The ideal length of each session is forty-five minutes to an hour. The problem is posed and people begin to produce ideas that someone writes down without prejudging the quality of them. Then, in another session, the ideas are reviewed and selected by a small group of specialists.

Group work requires three basic steps:

1) First contact and elimination of prejudice. (The understanding that the creative team of an advertising agency achieved after several months of working together should be achieved here in several hours or several days. And for that we need the intervention of a psychologist that

animates the group, acting as a catalyst between them.)

2) Imaginative step. (Freedom of ideas, without criticism, no matter how absurd those ideas are).

3) Review and selection. (Each idea is examined in detail and its ability to solve the problem is looked at).

The group is extremely critical, thus preventing mistakes. The group is a social stimulus that satisfies the need for communication, which is essential for the intellectual balance of a researcher.

The group maintains its creative enthusiasm, which often abandons an isolated individual when a momentary failure appears in his work. And finally, the group is a superior psychic force that prevents the excessive passion of each component, since ideas come from the group and not the individuals that form it.

Associative techniques

Gordon's synectic theory is notable among these techniques. Gordon says that by knowing the creation mechanism, the creative potential is increased. Artistic and scientific creations are of the same nature and are made by the same psychological processes. These processes are analogous in an individual or in a group, but the group has an accelerating effect for the production of ideas.

In order to artificially create these processes of creation, it proposes a:

Personal analogy: The creative must get under the skin of the object or product that it is studying and to try to examine the problem from the perspective of the object.

Direct analogy: To compare the problem with similar situations in other sciences, especially biology.

Unreal Analogy: To imagine the problem already solved and to dream the ideal solution.

Symbolic analogy: To find a picture that summarizes the problem.

Master techniques

The division: Divide the problem in all its parts (technological, financial, aesthetic, etc.) and try to find the solution for each of them in isolation.

Morphological techniques

The total solution (Zwicky): Zwicky is a Swiss citizen that immigrated to America. With his method, he made original discoveries about galaxies and propulsion systems, making important contributions in launching projectiles into space.

Zwicky´s method aims to find all possible solutions to a problem. It proposes carrying out four phases:

1) Establish a general problem statement. (Example: If you want to investigate a mixer, do not set a vegetables mixer as a target, but to address the problem in broader terms: "Invent a device to mix things up in the kitchen.")

2) Select the important parameters on which the solution will depend. (Example: blend modes, energy type, containers, etc.)

3) Each parameter offers several possible solutions which must then be combined with other parameters. At the end there are a very high number of possible solutions.

4) Evaluate the solutions in terms of their application, cost, demand of the market, etc.

3.3 Creative philosophies of the agencies

The philosophies of the great creative agencies are the answers to two important factors:

- The need to create a style, a personality that distinguishes the agency from all others.

-Personality (genius-individuality) of the creative team, which makes their image stronger than the image of the agency in which they work.

-The philosophies of agencies are an attempt to be different and to defend themselves from the others. They aim to personalize the way each agency works in order to subtract personality from each of its individual members, for the benefit of the overall image of the whole company; an image and a working system that could also be exported anywhere in the world, regardless of the geographical, social, economic and human situation of each country.

USP (Unique selling proposition)

The Unique Selling Proposition is the first and most important creative philosophy known. It was developed by Rosser Reeves in the early 1940s. Reeves was a Copywriter and the President of American agency Ted Bates.

The starting point is that Reeves considers humans, in relation to consumption, as rational beings that, when they make a purchase, they only seek a material gain. He therefore considers that logic, reasoning and a unique tangible benefit are the best means to persuade.

This material benefit must be communicated through advertising, with the following factors:

- The promise must be easy to remember.

- The benefit must be unique with respect to competitive products.

- It must be convincing, credible and rational.

- The communication of this benefit must be repeated, while the characteristics of the formula or product are not altered.

To find the USP, the promise to all the consumers possessing all these qualities, Reeves suggests:

- Considering the real benefits of the product.

- Creating (or discovering) a new advantage.

-Taking exclusive advantage of the common benefit with competitive products that has not been exploited by any of them.

With regards to brands, Reeves also thinks that a consumer's memory capacity is limited and, therefore, if our product and our communication occupy a part of their memory, that part will not be used for competition.

In 1961 Rosser Reeves's book "Reality in Advertising" was published, where his philosophy is developed in depth.

4D Plan

This is the philosophy used by Lintas advertising agency. Their name (4D) is determined by the four dimensions that the job of an advertising agency has according to Lintas. These dimensions are interdependent, and none is important if it is not in relation to others.

First dimension: Identify the unique selling idea or particular need of the consumer that the product satisfies.

Second dimension: Find the most compelling and effective presentation of this idea.

Third dimension: Find the best ways to communicate the idea.

Fourth dimension: Before and after the advertisement appears, remove uncertainty about its effectiveness as much as possible.

This philosophy, which is based on Reeves´s USP, however, differs greatly from it because it includes consumers in its approaches.

Working Principles

The 4D Plan provides a number of development principles to be followed when working in each of the dimensions.

First dimension

1) Understanding the needs and consumer attitudes.
2) Consider what competitors offer and compare it to what our product can offer.
3) Clearly define what our product offers and to whom.

Second Dimension

1) Be aware of the problem of getting the viewer's attention and to spark their interest.
2) Getting across a clear, distinctive, credible and convincing message in terms of the consumer.
3) Create a complete identity in all the material material and highlight the brand name.

Third Dimension

1) Select the appropriate media for the audience.
2) Select the appropriate media depending on the message.

3) Select the media with greater impact as a result of its power of penetration in the audience.

Fourth Dimension

1 Define clearly what is going to be measured.

2 Be creative in the use of research techniques.

3 Present clear results to help make decisions.

Working Documents:

For the best application of the principles of work and to not forget any of the steps you can use some documents, the most important being

Advertising brief: Defining the problem, or, in other words, the briefing that we already know.

Copy strategy: A document that summarizes the first dimension: what will we say? Defining it as follows:

- Basic consumer benefit: The benefit.

- Reason why: The reason for that benefit.

- Supporting evidence: The evidence supporting the benefit.

Media strategy: It is the end result of the work of the third dimension, the media strategy.

Creative expression: It is a document that Creative Directors elaborate in which they expose the reasons as to why they have chosen the forms of expression that will explain the campaign.

Creative Rationale

It is the creative philosophy of McCann Erickson, developed in 1970 by Ronnie Kirkwood, Creative Director of McCann London at that time.

The basic difference between Ronnie Kirkwood's Creative Rationale and Rosser Reeves's USP is that Kirkwood accepts the presence of emotional-irrational factors in the consumer's buying decisions.

Moreover, Kirkwood thinks that the USP tends to put the emphasis on the interest of the manufacturer rather than the consumer interest.

The USP suggests: "Here is a reason why you should buy this product" instead of "Here is a way that this product can help you to satisfy your needs."

The USP emphasizes the physical attributes of the product, using rational arguments and ignoring the fact that the sociological and psychological needs of the consumer are very important, on occasions even more than purely physical or physiological needs.

For Kirkwood, the communication of advertising works by creating, reinforcing or changing attitudes towards a product.

Kirkwood establishes four levels of the awareness of the advertising message by each receptor: what you know, what you think, what you feel and what you believe about the product.

What we know: It's what you know on a rational level, which is related to the physical attributes of the product.

What we think: The logical and rational interpretation of what you know about the product.

What we feel: The emotional interpretation of what you know about the product.

What we believe: Is that what you are convinced about. In fact, the difference between "feel" and "believe" depends on the intensity of the feeling.

"Creative Rationale" is a document that establishes a work discipline that requires everyone involved in creating the campaign following what is established in its philosophy. Ronnie Kirkwood thinks about a very short document to be completed from the briefing given by the client, and the content will not be altered as long as the changing factors or existing marketing objectives at the time of preparation don't change.

This document consists of the following parts:

1) A front page which indicates the customer's name, the name of the product , the media channel used (if known in advance) and the duration of the campaign.

2) Target audience, which specifies if the target is a buyer or a consumer, setting its sociological characteristics and personality as well as their behavior, customs and habits regarding the product.

3) Attitudes and opinions existing in the target audience about the brand at the present time, ie, before the campaign. What they know, what they think, what they feel and what they believe.

4) Attitudes and opinions existing in the target audience about competitive brands and products, expressed in the same terms (know, think, feel and believe) and relating the three or four most important brands in the market share.

5) What attitudes or opinions existing in the target audience regarding our product should be strengthened, modified or changed?

6) Desired consumer response: What do we want our target audience to know, think, feel and believe about our product, once it has been exposed to the marketing communication that our campaign will set?

7) The concept: What is the basic selling idea over which advertising will be built, and that will cause the desired consumer response?

Paragraphs 1 to 5 must be completed by the accounts department of the agency, and it is down to those responsible for creativity to respond to paragraphs 6 and 7.

Creative advertising philosophies today

The USP, 4D Creative Plan and Creative Rationale are just a few examples, the most important, of the many creative philosophies that large multinational agencies developed between the forties and the seventies. Most agencies developed their own philosophies of work, which, with minor differences, could all fit within any of the three mentioned in this chapter.

Today, almost all of these approaches are not in use, or are only applicable to certain types of products. The reason for this is that all creative philosophies are based on product differentiation, when most of these currently have no differences.

The improvement of technology has led to products being increasingly similar, making it impossible to establish objective differences between them. And this has led to advertising trying to find the difference in the emotional aspects of the communication itself; so that the customer relationship is established on terms of complicity, trying to obtain his empathy towards the product and the brand through a game of intelligence, rather than a concrete proposal for benefits.

PRODUCTION

4.1 Audiovisual Production

To turn creative ideas into concrete materials, into communication pieces that we know as adverts, a long process known as production is required. In the case of audiovisual production, this process begins when the creative group materializes ideas into a radio script, a storyboard for a TV spot, an Internet video or any other audiovisual media.

Radio scripts

In a radio script, the copywriter writes the words that the speaker will read, as well as technical specifications regarding the music or special effects. Once the script is approved by the client, it goes on to be recorded, using a recording studio and a sound technician.

In advertising agencies, the media production department is responsible for hiring the studio and providing a selection of speakers, using the most appropriate voice for each occasion. Once the recording is done and copies are sent to each radio station, the media department is responsible for distributing them according to the plan.

TV spots and other videos

In the case of television, the process is more complex and requires the participation of a greater number of specialists. The creative group transforms its ideas into a story board that is used to present it to the client. The story board is a script organized in the form of illustrations, which tries to display the different situations that make up the film. Below each illustration the copywriter adds a brief description of the image, and an explanation of the intended movement of the camera.

Naturally, there is a huge difference between a story board and the end product. A great effort of imagination is required by the customer to approve the ideas in the story board stage. In any case, both the creative team and the client will closely follow the whole production process in order to ensure that the initial idea is developed successfully.

The audiovisual production department of an agency requests a budget from two or three production companies to undertake the completion of the spot. These companies are independent and work with all advertising agencies. The main focus of these companies is established by a filmmaker (equivalent to a conventional film director) and a production manager. They also have a large team of production assistants, decorators, stylists, makeup artists, electricians, etc... A photography director, hired for each occasion, is also required.

After selecting the production company and approving the budget, a pre-production meeting, attended by the creative agency, the client's representative and the director and producer of the production company, takes place. At this meeting the casting (models or actors), location (place where the shooting will take place), costumes, sets, etc., as well as the timing of production is defined. The following steps will be the shooting of the film, edition of different shots, the sound and post-production processes necessary to reach the copy-standard or first copy, from which all the other necessary copies for various television channels will be take place.

4.2 Graphic production

Final Arts

When creativity is intended for print, the first step in the execution of ideas is the sketch: A graphic design, very similar to what the final advert will be, which enables the client to get a very real idea. Today, thanks to the the valuable contribution of the Mac (Macintosh computers), sketches are so perfect that sometimes they are more colorful even than the advert itself. But the sketch, as such, can not be sent to the media. It also requires a finalization process to become an artwork, or digital materials that can be reproduced by the media.

In between the sketch and final art sometimes there are photographs or original illustrations. In these cases, the graphic production department will contact the most appropriate providers, manage budgets and select the appropriate professionals to carry out the work at the disposition of the creative group. After creating the photographs or illustrations and typography, logos, etc., they proceed to complete the final art that will be delivered to the media for diffusion.

Brochures and billboards

In the case of different print media to the press or magazines, the agency is also responsible for performing the necessary photomechanical processes and overseeing all development of the material until it is printed. The Art Director of the agency supervises the photomechanical tests, so that all materials (brochures, billboards, etc.), are finished with optimal print quality.

ANNEX I

TELEVISION ADVERTISING

In Spain, television was the king of media from 1970 to 1990 with only two channels, TVE's first and second channel, which monopolized the market, reaching audiences of more than 50% of the total population of our country. With just one pass in the first channel on Friday night, you could reach virtually 90% of any target group.

That golden age of television was also reflected in advertising agencies, concentrating their budgets on that media channel (up to 80% of the entire buget in some agencies) and applied their creative efforts almost exclusively on developing TV spots.

As a result of this dominance of television over other media, during the eighties the Spanish advertising industry reached a large worldwide notoriety for its brilliant creativity in television, winning many awards in the best festivals in the world, such as Cannes, London or New York, and positioning itself as the third global advertising power, after the United Kingdom and the United States.

Today, with the arrival in 1990 of private channels, the scenarion is complicated, scattering the audience and decreasing the effectiveness of advertising in that medium. As a result of this, the importance of television as an advertising medium has been reduced in favor of other media, especially new media, which in recent years has seen strong growth in advertising spending.

ANNEX II

ADVERTISING PRINT MEDIA

Qualitatively speaking, print media has always been the ugly duckling of Spanish advertising. The great importance of television as an advertising medium has predominantly relegated other media channels for many years, forcing them to take a back seat in the interests of the agency and creative people.

In the case of print media, creative teams simply put across a reminder of TV adverts. They translate the TV spot to the press, magazines or external supports (cabins, hoarding, marquees, etc.), using one of its most characteristic images and a brief summary of its speech. They try to remind the print media reader of the message that they already knew through television, ignoring not only the appropriate conceptual idea for each medium, but also the aduate graphics for the specific message.

In the last years of the twentieth century the situation changed substantially. Faced with the loss of effectiveness of television, print media was favored by investments. And consequently, agencies and creative people paid much more attention to adverts for these supports.

The improvement of creativity was evident, as proved by the many awards earned by Spanish graphics in major competitions throughout the world.

ANNEX III

INTERNET ADVERTISING

The real media revolution has taken place with the arrival of Internet in the last years of the twentieth century, and especially with the emergence of social networks, starting in 2004.

The consumer, or advertising message receiver, has become critical in the process, because now they are able to interact with the sender and also exchange their impressions of the product with other consumers. Commercial breaks are giving way to an engagement advertising where the message is fused with the content of the media.

These changes are still being assimilated by the advertising industry, which is in a constant process of transformation. Creative people from the television generation, still at the peak of the industry, must give way in the coming years to the generation of digital natives.

THE MEDIA

The media is a vehicle that advertising agencies use to establish contacts with the consumer. Any vehicle capable of containing an advertising message automatically becomes a media channel. And it is virtually impossible to give a full relation of the possible media, because, as you can imagine, many vehicles can be used as advertising media, from a simple folder to an aerostatics balloon, or the side of a bus.

In this chapter I will refer exclusively to popular media, which are most commonly used by advertising agencies and constitute over 80 per cent of advertising's investment worldwide.

5.1 Ranking

There are three basic characteristics of the media, which can be classified: the general content, the format and the advertising content.

General content

Taking into account only its general content, advertising media can be classified into three categories:

-Information media (TV, radio, newspapers and magazines, both paper and digital formats)

 -Social media (Cinema, video, Internet, etc.)

- Advertising media (Outdoor advertising, direct advertising and point of sale material).

The relationship this media has with advertising is determined by the following variables:

Information media

-They are financed by advertising

-Advertising is conditioned by the special structure of the media (color, formats, etc.)

-The information competes with advertising.

-They're seen, heard or read by one sole consumer at a time (seen, read or heard in intimacy)

Social media

-They are not financed by advertising.

-They have a heterogeneous audience.

-They compete with advertising.

-They determine the structure of adverts.

Advertising media

-They are created by and for advertising.

-Of a variable structure (adapted to your needs)

-They don't contain anything other than advertising.

Form

Depending on its form, advertising media can be classified into two categories:

-Print media: Newspapers, magazines, outdoor advertising, direct mail and point of sale material.
-Audiovisual and digital media: Cinema, television, radio, internet.

Content

In relation to the advertising content, the media can be classified into two categories:

-Conceptual media: Television, cinema, radio, outdoor advertising and point of sale.

-Argument media: Newspapers, magazines and direct mail.

5.2 Features

Television
According to the above classifications, television is a medium of visual and conceptual information. Its specific features are:

-National coverage

-Great audience

-Very cheap cost per thousand impacts

-Used as basic media in national campaigns

-Short-messages (20, 30 or 45 seconds).

-Usually TV shootings are in 35 mm, like in the movies. Lately they're also in digital video.

-A technique of close up and medium shots, appropriate to the size of the screen.

Cinema

According to the rankings, cinema is a social, conceptual and visual media. Its features are:

-National coverage.

-Little audience and very heterogeneous (conditioned by the film shown).

-High cost per thousand impacts.

-Long messages compared to television.

-Big Screen (not a slave to close ups).

-Direct contract process or through exclusivists.

Newspapers

Newspapers are a news medium. They're also a print and argumental medium, and their specific features are:

-Local/regional (in most cases).

-Little Audience (mostly masculine).

-Massive use of black and white.

-Fleeting Message (read and discarded).

Magazines

We must distinguish three types of magazines: general content, female and specialized information. The first two groups have a national reach, while the latter group includes all kinds of varieties, from local topics (schools magazines, neighborhood associations, religious, etc.) to national subjects (engineering, economics, motoring, sports, etc.). All of them have some common features besides being cases of information, printed and argumental media:

-Massive use of color.

-Permanence of the message (the magazine is conserved for some time and reread several times).

- Less flexible formats than advertising in newspapers.

    - Homogeneous audience, focused mainly on every specific subject.

Radio

Radio is an information, audiovisual and ambivalent medium with regards to the third classification, because it is conceptual, when it comes to adverts, and argumental when it comes to programs. The most important characteristics of this medium, from a strictly advertising point of view are:

-Local or regional media generally. Only reaches national audience when a station sets up a hook-up transmission.

-It has a low cost per thousand, enabling a high frequency.

-Personal and intimate media. It speaks to the individual and not the crowd.

-Flexible, allowing the broadcast of advertising spots, jingles or programs. Outdoor Advertising

Outdoor media

Following the above classifications, it is strictly an advertising, printed and conceptual medium. It is virtually impossible to define the physical characteristics of a type of outdoor advertising media, because it is likely to take up all kinds of shapes, whose only common denominator is always being located in the street or in places with large crowds.

The most important features of outdoor advertising are:

-Usually used as a means of support due to their space limitations.

-The message should be brief (conceptual).

-It must be treated with very strong graphics to make an immediate impact.

-It's essentially a local media.

Internet

We can regard Internet as a media channel, but its versatile use turns it into a different format every time. In Internet we can find classic classified ads (Google Adwords), or modern formats of Branded Content, similar to a film in short format. There are also conventional television advertisements inserted on platforms like Youtube, or exclusive special formats used in social networks.

This type of media is particularly suitable for the transmission of content that supports the management of a brand's personality.

ANNEX

Diffusion measurement systems, audience and investments in advertising media.

When planning advertising campaigns in different media, it is absolutely essential to have some tools, beyond those provided by the media, able to guide planners and provide the work with the greatest amount of objectivity. Every country has these kinds of organizations. For example, following I have listed some companies that provide the most reliable diffusion data, segmentation of audiences and advertising investments that brands perform in the media in Spain nowadays.

OJD (Diffusion justification office).

It dates back to October 1964, since when it has provided information on the emission, diffusion and sale of all printed publications. Currently it has about 700 publications, with over 1,000 annual verifications, because magazines that have a circulation of over 25,000 copies are verified two times per year. Its ownership structure is formed by advertising agencies, publishers, advertisers, and professional associations in these fields. The largest number of partners come from the media, since it is made up of over 100 supports.

The research methodology consists of an accounting and administrative audit that verifies all documents in the printing process, from the purchase of paper to the final sale at the kiosk.

In May 1997, the OJD implemented a web measurement service that controlled websites, certifying the number of visits and number of monthly page views. Today, this service which is still active has the power to control numerous specific audiences on Internet, such as the infamous Google Analytics.

EGM (General Media Study)

In 1968, a collective of advertising agencies, advertisers and media conducted the first study on media audiences. This study was managed by an independent research institute and formally validated by AEA (Spanish Association of Advertisers), although in the early years it had no legal identity.

In 1975 the EGM company, which in 1988 was renamed AIMC (Association for Media Research) was legally established. Currently it has about 200 members among media agencies, advertising agencies, advertisers, media and several others, among which is the General Society of Authors of Spain (SGAE).

This is a non-profit association and its main activity is to conduct the general media research. The study is based on a platform of 32,500 personal interviews throughout Spain (except Ceuta and Melilla), with people aged fourteen or over, representing the entire Spanish population.

The interviews are conducted during the first, second and fourth quarter of each year, and each of these three periods include a field work of eight weeks.

Kantar Media (TV audit))

Radio Televisión Española (public company) convened in 1986 a competition to measure their audiences which was won by the company Ecotel, which were the first panel in 1988. In 1990, with the birth of private television channels, a second panel was developed by the company Media Control. In 1992, Sofres bought both companies, Ecotel and Media Control, fusing them into one. Later in 1998, Sofres associates with Taylor Nelson AGB multinational, leading to the creation of Taylor Nelson Sofres. In 2010 the company changed its name to Kantar Media.

The method developed by this company is based on a device that is managed via the remote control every time a family member switches or switches off the TV. There is a permanent platform of 4,625 households with over 10,000 individuals, scattered throughout the country.
The devices are connected to all television sets and videos of every home, and all individuals aged four or

bove are identified. A total of 5,500 television sets and 2,500 videos are audited in over 1,300 municipalities in Spain.

It is a sophisticated system that can supply all kinds of audience data in real time, which is extremely useful not only for agency planners, but also for TV channel programmers themselves.

Infoadex

Infoadex is a private company founded in 1994 with 50% of the shares distributed between AC Nielsen, SA and Triplo, SA. Its objective is to monitor and analyse advertising in the media, providing investment data of different brands and products, grouped by sectors in each of the analyzed media. Infoadex also provides copies of adverts in media, which, together with the economic investment, enables a reliable reconstruction of the competition's campaigns.

Advertising investment in Spain, measured by Infoadex in 2013 reached 10,400 million euros, of which 4.200 million is conventional advertising (newspapers, magazines, radio, cinema, television and outdoor), and the rest is non-conventional media, most notably the Internet, with 21% of the total investment.

BELOW THE LINE

Below the line is the set of all the communication activities that take place outside of the major mass media. The most representative are sales promotion, direct marketing, public relations, sponsoring, events and merchandising. All these activities, just like advertising, are used to communicate with the consumer, in order to convey specific aspects of the brand or product. In some cases, such as public relations, sponsorship, or sponsoring events, it is reinforcing the image; and in others, such as promotion, direct marketing and merchandising goals it is more related to the immediate purchase of the product.

In this chapter we will deal in more detail the three below the line activities that are most important in relation to investments: sales promotion, direct marketing and merchandising.

6.1 Sales promotion

Sales promotion is a marketing activity that aims to stimulate demand for a product or service for use or consumption by the final consumer or to encourage rotation through distribution channels.

Promotional strategies

Although the ultimate goal of every sales promotion is the same, marketing situations that give rise to the need for a promotion may be very different. So we can say that each responds to a different promotion strategy, or, in other words, tends to solve different problems.

- Removal of factory stocks due to:

- Problems of storage

- Change in pack design

- Change in the formula of the product

- Elimination of stocks of wholesalers and retailers, to make way for new sales.

- Overload of stocks of wholesalers and retailers to stop sales of the competition.

- Support new product launches.

<u>- Need for rapid consumption of perishable products.</u>

Promotional target group

As a result of the different promotional strategies, the target group of the promotions is also different:

- Sellers (Own sales force or wholesales)

- Wholesales

- Retailers

-Consumers

The different promotions are carried out having each of these groups as targets separately, or several of them, or all at once on global strategies.

Promotions for sellers, wholesalers and retailers

In every promotion there is an economic part and an emotional part: the economic part is determined by the worth of the gift, the offer or the percentage given to the receiver of the promotion; and the emotional part is determined by the way it must be used in each case to access the gift.

Naturally, the gift's possibilities are endless, and so is the way to access them; so, here we will just select the most common formulas in each of the receiver groups, distinguishing between proposal and promotion mechanics formulas.

Sellers promotion

- Bonus in product, independent from the normal commission of every seller

- Gift items

- Travels

<u>Used procedures</u>

- Simple share sales

- Scale share sales

- Contests

Wholesalers and retailers promotion

They are usually very similar to the promotions of the sellers themselves, with the same type of benefits and the same procedures.

- Discounts in invoice

- Gifting products

- Gifting objects

- Travels

Consumer promotions

No doubt, consumer promotions are the most frequent and the most numerous. Although the procedures are usually very similar in all cases, the emotional aspect is varied and depends on the type of product or service.

Here we will only explain the promotions and procedures applied to consumer products that, as a result of their common characteristics can be applied to a wide variety of products in all kinds of markets.

On pack

The name "on pack" is given to all those promotions in which the object that is gifted is outside of product packaging. This requires changing the packaging or additional packaging to integrate the promotion gift. The gift must be very well presented, so that your image is not to the detriment of the product. The item that is given must be practical and desirable for the consumer, because having it in sight, accepting or rejecting it a priori has an enormous influence on the purchase.

The possible disadvantage of a promotion like this is that by requiring a new packaging for the gift, it could become very expensive. And on the other hand, if the image of the gift isn't looked after very well, it could harm the image of the product.

In pack

The gift is inside the packaging of the product, (for example inside a detergent drum). The essential condition is that the gift is something known by the consumer, so you can awaken a desire for it.

The advantage of this type of promotion with regard to the "on pack" is that, by not requiring new packaging, the costs are lower.

Banded pack

Two products of the same company being sold together. It is a kind of promotion widely used to launch a new product, which therefore rests on the good image of the other products from the same company. The approach of the offer in this promotion has two possibilities: a) One of the products is given free when the client buys the other. b) If you buy them together, the price of both is lowered.

The essential condition is that at least one of the two products needs to be well known. The advantage is that it makes ordinary consumers of the known product try the new product. The disadvantage is that it is a very expensive promotion (packaging, supply, etc.) and, if the quality of the new product does not meet the user requirements, the image of both products may deteriorate.

Self Liquidating

This promotion consists in selling your product with a gift, significantly reducing the price of the latter. This gift should be complementary with the product or have a connection with it. It should be very easy to evaluate, so that the buyer can appreciate the savings he's made, or also very difficult to assess, because it is an object that can not be acquired on the market.

The cost of this type of promotion is very small, and sometimes even free.

Sampling

It is a miniature distribution of the product. It is mostly used for new products whose quality is visibly evident in a sample.

It has the advantage of ensuring a test of the product and the disadvantage that the cost is very high, due to the distribution and the need for special packaging.

Couponing

These are typical discount vouchers of a certain amount. They are used especially for consumer products (food and cleaning, mainly). They don't include any gifts and only offer a small percentage of the commercial benefit of the product. It is a kind of promotion that is very suitable for retailers to eliminate stocks. The main disadvantage is the high cost of the deal, and the appearance of rogue retailers, who can take advantage of a product's vouchers to sell some of its competition's products.

Demonstrations and tastings

Demonstrations and tastings are carried out at the point of sale, in order to get an instant purchase of the product. It is a very expensive type of promotion; it also requires the product to have real quality, and for that quality to really set it apart from competing products.

6.2 Direct marketing

Direct marketing, also known as direct mail, is any communication that is aimed at a personalized receiver, ie, at a particular and localized target. It is specifically an advertising media. And as in the case of outdoor advertising, we can not speak of a specific material that groups all the features of direct marketing, because what defines advertising media is precisely its vast possibilities for formats and physical supports .

Key Features:

-Very flexible media in terms of formats, designs, etc.

-Generally it is a complementary support for campaigns in mass media.

- Widely used for sampling and promotional coupons because of its access to highly localized targets.

Direct Marketing procedures are usually based on a method that is known by the name of AIDA, an acronym that responds to the following:

- Call reader **A**ttention.

- Awaken her **I**nterest.

-Incite the **D**esire.

-Invite to the **A**ction.

The short-term efficiency of Direct Marketing, compared to conventional advertising, has led to it being developed dramatically in recent years, reaching a total investment similar to the total of mass media in developed countries.

Also their formats, that in the past focused mainly on the mailing of letters and brochures, have been refined and extended to other types of "face to face" demonstrations, such as roadshows, telephone marketing , emails, etc.

6.3 Merchandising

As we noted in the chapter on "Structures and business relationships', Merchandising is any activity that takes place within the point of sale to promote the product display.

There are some classics advertising materials that are used relatively frequently in all Merchandising activities. The most common are the following:

Display

An element, usually made of cardboard or plastic, placed on a display on a counter. It is normally supported by a pedestal and is used to display the product and the theme of the advertising campaign photographically.

Display-exhibitor

Similar to the previous element, but on this occasion it is usually made of metal or plastic. Apart from the functions of the display, it serves as support for a certain amount of products.

Window bill

This is the classic sticker -small in size- on windows or entrances to shops.

Self talker

Small sized "talkers" placed next to the product on the shelves, directing consumer attention towards the product.

Crowner

A cardboard element with many faces which is placed on large products, using the product itself as support.

Posters

Of different sizes, made out of paper or plastic and glued to the wall. They are also used to announce promotions to consumers at the point of sale.

Headboards

Headboards are tower products, normally on offer, which are located in the corridors of large supermarkets. Company sales reps, or any people hired specifically for this purpose, are responsible for the maintenance of these materials in stores and also for trying to boost its visibility.
It is also part of the work of merchandising to take care of the product on the shelf, keeping it clean and visible, removing the damaged units and ensuring the stock of the product at all times.

NEW TECHNOLOGIES

The technological revolution that has occurred since the birth of the Internet has transformed the business world, giving rise to a new economic order in which the media plays an important role. Advertising in general has benefited from the emergence of new brands that need to develop their image with consumers, but they are also being affected by the structural changes that have come with new technological supports, which the strategy and the agency's creativity must adapt to.

7.1 Internet

It's among the most revolutionary new technologies. It is a computer network that is able to connect in real time with all inhabitants of the globe, wherever they are. This network skips all boundaries and enables not only the unlimited extension of traditional commerce, but also the creation of new forms of trade that are exclusive to this new medium.

Over 800 million web pages are currently recognized in the world and over 2,500 million users. And the numbers continue to grow.

Internet advertising, also called on-line advertising, has just begun its journey, but it has its own language and unique features that testify to what will be its powerful evolution in the future. The main elements of Internet advertising in the early years were the website, the banner and e-mail. But nowadays social networks receive the greatest part of advertising investments.

The "website"

The presentation letter of a company or an individual on the Internet is called a website, also known as a web page, and it is a kind of interactive e-brochure through which you can communicate anything from written information to complex audiovisual content.

For a website to stand out it must be included in major search engines and promoted both in traditional media and in the network itself.

The "banner"

Today, a banner is the most widespread ad format online, although its effectiveness has decreased significantly in recent years. It's like a small window which opens on the home page of a website which gives you access to information about a product or service.

The banner should be simple but very attractive, thereby enticing the Internet user to click on it and visit its content.

The "e-mail"

Perhaps the most popular use on the Internet and the fastest growing is the e-mail or email.

It is estimated that there are currently more than 250,000 million e-mails sent or received each day worldwide. And many of them are exclusively advertising content.

7.2 Interactive TV

The integration of televisions and computers results in interactive televisions: a system that allows us, without leaving our homes, to participate in contests or games, send and receive messages, buy all kinds of objects and information in real time.

An interactive advertisement, for example, will let us know instantly where it was filmed, how you can get there, what is the current weather in that place, what designer is the dress the model is wearing, where the closest store to our house that sells it is and even if they have our size available.

Television allows us now access the Internet via remote control and interact with the information on the screen with the touch of a button. The possibilities of advertising development of this new medium are awesome, and will force agencies to find new creative formats, beyond the traditional spot.

7.3 Social media

No doubt, social media is now the fastest growing advertising medium which has the brightest future for asvertisers. The content on Youtube and interaction with consumers through Facebook and other similar networks enables companies to develop brand strategies and e-commerce, with an unknown emotional involvement until now.

However, it is a type of advertising that has a low record of effectiveness. Advertising companies still don't handle the communication mechanisms that this new media requires.

7.4 Smartphones

So-called smart phones, which have become a natural extension of man and that are by our side 24 hours a day, are the backbone of what is now known as Internet 3.0. Intelligent networking, via mobile, will manage most of our movements in the future.

Already more than 1,500 million applications exist for Iphone and Android systems, through which we can get thousands of useful services and most of them for free. These applications are certainly a great advertising medium, but it is only the tip of the iceberg of what mobile phones can offer as media channels in the future.

ANNEX

THE FUTURE IS COMING

The development of advertising communication and the birth of new media and new technologies have dramatically changed the ways of reaching consumers. Today the advertising language seeks the complicity of the receptor in an intimate dialogue from person to person.

From Persuasion to Complicity

In advertising, like in fashion, there are cyclical trends. Today you wear a long skirt, tomorrow shorts skirts are in. Today adverts are in color, tomorrow they'll be in black and white. But major changes only occur once in a while. In the last fifty years, fashion has gone from a formal rigidness to an anarchy of "dress however you want". And advertising has stopped looking to persuade, instead aiming to achieve the complicity of the receptor.

Today, adverts are more emotional than informational, and are directed at a mature audience that knows the mechanism of advertising very well. New consumers look for a sense of humor, spectacle, beauty and intelligence in an advert.

They know the game and love to play as equals; not to be persuaded but to take part in the communication, developing a genuine empathy with brands.

From mass to personal

The technological revolution has been transforming the news media for decades by bringing them closer every day to a defined and specific consumer whose personal interests are the focus of all commercial strategies.

Magazines paved the way, followed by FM radio stations, cable and satellite television channels and eventually Internet. In all cases, the common denominator is an increasingly individualized offer. Radio formulas, with their special music for each target, thematic channels and Internet connections that identify the user's profile with absolute precision, all media evolve from mass audiences to an effective and indiscriminate intimacy with the consumer, through an increasingly personal communication.

www.ingramcontent.com/pod-product-compliance
Lightning Source LLC
Chambersburg PA
CBHW081313170526
45166CB00011B/3507